P9-CDS-672

WHAT DOES A
POLICE OFFICER DO?

What Does a Community Helper Do?   Felicia Lowenstein

Words to Know

accident (ak-SIH-dent)—Something that happens that is not planned.

emergency (ee-MUR-jun-see)—Something that happens that needs quick action.

equipment (e-KWIP-ment)—The tools used for a certain activity.

laws (lawz)—Rules that a country or a group of people agree to follow.

police officer (poh-LEES OFF-e-sur)—A man or woman trained to keep us safe.

sirens (SIGH-runz)—The loud alarm turned on in a police car.

Enslow Elementary

an imprint of

Enslow Publishers, Inc.

E

40 Industrial Road
Box 398
Berkeley Heights, NJ 07922
USA

PO Box 38
Aldershot
Hants GU12 6BP
UK

http://www.enslow.com

Contents

"Calling Bravo One."
"10-2, Bravo One here. Over."
"We have a 10-40 on I-95 at Main Street. An overturned tractor trailer. They're going to need some help. Over."

Answering a Call

"10-4, we'll be right there."

If you guessed that this was two police officers talking on a police radio, you are right! Every day police officers talk this way. They say "10-2" to mean "We hear you." They say "10-40" for a car or truck accident. Police officers help people like you and me.

Police officers help us and keep us safe.

Where Do Police Officers Work?

Police officers can work for your town or state. Their job is to keep you safe. Police officers make sure people obey the laws.

Training is important in becoming a police officer.

Who Can Be Police Officers?

Police officers can be men or women. To be a police officer, you must have special training. You also must go to a special school. Men and women learn how to run fast, shoot a gun, save a life, and keep you safe.

gun

gloves

handcuffs

pepper spray

radio

baton

flashlight

ammunition

Police officers wear uniforms like this one.

What Do Police Officers Wear?

Police officers wear uniforms. Sometimes they also wear plain clothes. They carry special tools.

lights

Call 911 in an emergency

name of police department

computer monitor   radar

switches for lights and sirens

radio   keyboard

Police cars have a lot of equipment in them.

Inside a Police Car

Look at the outside and inside of the police car. The outside has lights that flash. It has the name of the police department. It says to call 9-1-1 in an emergency. The inside has special equipment that help a police officer. It has a computer and switches for the lights and sirens. What else can you find?

Different Jobs

Not all police officers do the same job. Some watch for unsafe driving. Others solve crimes. Still others give first aid. You may see police officers on bicycles, on horseback, or working with police dogs. Together the whole team keeps you safe.

Before they start their day, police
officers hear a report.

When Do Police Officers Work?

Police officers work days and nights. They always start the same way. They hear a report about what happened before they came to work.

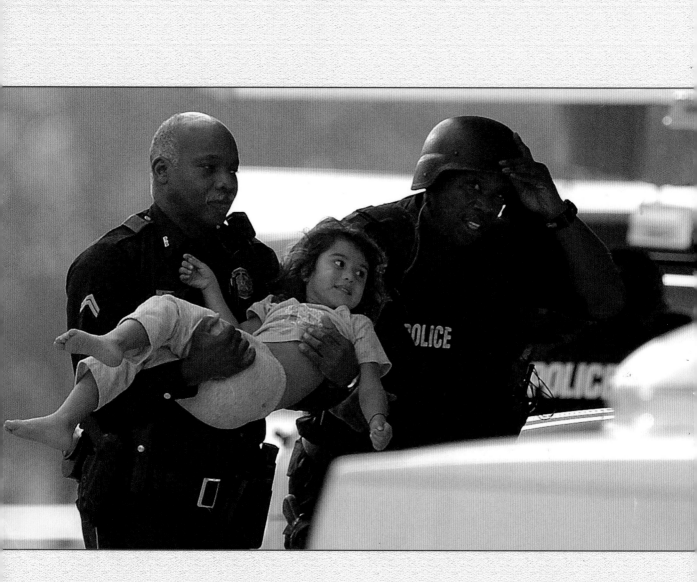

Police work is not easy. Police officers have to be ready for anything.

Police Work Is Hard

Police work is not safe or easy. Police officers can be hurt. They have to act fast. They need to work hard, for long hours.

Every day police officers help us. Some get awards for doing something brave.

Police Officers Are Heroes

Some police officers get medals. They did something brave. Most people say: All police officers are community heroes.

Fingerprinting

Police officers use fingerprints to help them solve crimes. Did you know that everyone's fingerprints are different? Take a look at your fingertips. Do you see the little lines and swirls? That is your fingerprint.

Take your own fingerprints. It is easy.

You will need:
- two index cards
- a sharpened pencil
- clear tape

1. Rub the pencil over the index card. Make a dark spot that is a little bigger than your fingertip. The darker you make it, the better your fingerprint will be.

2. Press one finger onto the spot. Try to press with the part that is near where it folds.

3. Then press your finger against the sticky side of the tape. The pencil marks should come off onto it.

4. Press the tape down on the second card to make your print. Write which hand and finger you used.

5. Try it again with your other fingers!

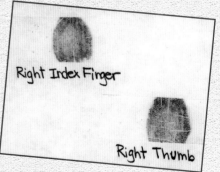

Right Index Finger

Right Thumb

Learn More

Books

Adamson, Heather. *A Day in the Life of a Police Officer*. Mankato, Minn.: Capstone Press, 2004.

Flanagan, Alice K. *Police Officers*. Minneapolis, Minn.: Compass Point Books, 2000.

Russell, Joan Plummer. *Aero and Officer Mike: Police Partners*. Honesdale, Penn.: Caroline House, Boyds Mills Press, 2001.

Simon, Charnon. *Police Officers*. Chanhassen, Minn.: Child's World, 2003.

Stille, Darlene R. *Police Cars*. Minneapolis, Minn.: Compass Point Books, 2003.

Internet Addresses

McGruff, the National Crime Prevention Council
<http://www.mcgruff.org>
Help the dog McGruff take a bite out of crime! This site has tips and games.

Who Dunnit?
<http://www.cyberbee.com/whodunnit/crime.html>
Click on "Fingerprinting" to learn more.

Index

Note to Teachers and Parents: The *What Does a Community Helper Do?* series supports curriculum standards for K–4 learning about community services and helpers. The Words to Know section introduces subject-specific vocabulary. Early readers may require help with these new words.

Series Literacy Consultant:
Allan A. De Fina, Ph.D.
Past President of the New Jersey Reading Association
Professor, Department of Literacy Education
New Jersey City University

Enslow Elementary, an imprint of Enslow Publishers, Inc.

Enslow Elementary® is a registered trademark
of Enslow Publishers, Inc.

Library of Congress Cataloging-in-Publication Data

Lowenstein, Felicia.
  What does a police officer do? / Felicia Lowenstein.
    p. cm. — (What does a community helper do?)
  Includes bibliographical references and index.
  ISBN 0-7660-2541-1
  1. Police—Juvenile literature. I. Title. II. Series.
HV7922.L68 2005
363.2'3—dc22
                                        2004006894

Printed in the United States of America

10 9 8 7 6 5 4 3 2 1

To Our Readers:
We have done our best to make sure all Internet Addresses in this book were active and appropriate when we went to press. However, the author and the publisher have no control over and assume no liability for the material available on those Internet sites or on other Web sites they may link to. Any comments or suggestions can be sent by e-mail to comments@enslow.com or to the address on the back cover.

Illustration Credits: Associated Press, pp. 1, 4, 6, 14 (top left and right), 16, 18, 20; Associated Press, Fremont Argus, p. 14 (bottom right); Associated Press, Hattiesburg American, p. 8; Associated Press, The Independent, p. 14 (bottom left); Enslow Publishers, Inc., p. 22 (top right and bottom right); © 2004 JupiterImages, p. 22 (bottom left); Courtesy of the North Plainfield (New Jersey) Police Department, pp. 2, 10, 12 (top and bottom).

Cover Illustration: Associated Press (bottom); Associated Press, top left to right (all).